♓ LOVE SIGNS ♓

PISCES

19 February – 20 March

JULIA & DEREK PARKER

DK

DORLING KINDERSLEY

London • New York • Stuttgart • Moscow

Dedicated to Martin Lethbridge

DK

A DORLING KINDERSLEY BOOK

Project Editor • Annabel Morgan
Art Editor • Anna Benjamin
Managing Editor • Francis Ritter
Managing Art Editor • Derek Coombes
DTP Designer • Cressida Joyce
Production Controller • Martin Croshaw

ACKNOWLEDGMENTS

Photography: Steve Gorton: pp. 10, 13–15, 17–19, 46–49; Ian O'Leary: 16. *Additional photography by:* Colin Keates, Dave King, Monique Le Luhandre, David Murray, Tim Ridley, Clive Streeter, Harry Taylor, Matthew Ward. *Artworks:* Nici Demin: 34–45; Peter Lawman: *jacket,* 4, 12; Paul Redgrave: 24–33; Satwinder Sehmi: *glyphs;* Jane Thomson: *borders;* Rosemary Woods: 11. Peter Lawman's paintings are exhibited by the Portal Gallery Ltd, London.

Picture credits: Bridgeman Art Library/Hermitage, St. Petersburg: 51; Robert Harding Picture Library: 20l, 20c, 20r; Images Colour Library: 9; The National Gallery, London: 11; The Royal Geographical Society: 48br; Tony Stone Images: 21t, 21b; The Victoria and Albert Museum, London: 5; Zefa: 21c.

Thanks to: Sarah Ashun, Emma Brogi, Charlie Chan, John Filbey, Jane Lawrie, Sharon Lucas, Daniel McCarthy, Marion McLornan, Christine Rista, Ola Rudowska, Tim Scott, Isobel Sinden, Martha Swift, Mark Thurgood, Cangy Venables *and* Liz Wagstaff.

First published in Great Britain in 1996 by
Dorling Kindersley Limited, 9 Henrietta Street, London WC2E 8PS

Copyright © 1996 Dorling Kindersley Limited, London
Text copyright © 1996 Julia and Derek Parker

Visit us on the World Wide Web at http://www.dk.com

A CIP catalogue record for this book is available from the British Library.

ISBN 0-7513-0332-1

Reproduced by Bright Arts, Hong Kong
Printed and bound by Imago, Hong Kong

CONTENTS

ASTROLOGY & YOU

THERE IS MUCH MORE TO ASTROLOGY THAN YOUR SUN SIGN.
A SIMPLE INVESTIGATION INTO THE POSITION OF THE OTHER
PLANETS AT THE MOMENT OF YOUR BIRTH WILL PROVIDE YOU
WITH FASCINATING INSIGHTS INTO YOUR PERSONALITY.

*Y*our birth sign, or Sun sign, is the sign of the zodiac that the Sun occupied at the moment of your birth. The majority of books on astrology concentrate only on explaining the relevance of the Sun signs. This is a simple form of astrology that can provide you with some interesting but rather general information about you and your personality. In this book, we take you a step further, and reveal how the planets Venus and Mars work in association with your Sun sign to influence your attitudes towards romance and sexuality.

In order to gain a detailed insight into your personality, a "natal" horoscope, or birth chart, is necessary. This details the position of all the planets in our solar system at the moment of your birth, not just the position of the Sun. Just as the Sun occupied one of the 12 zodiac signs when you were born, perhaps making you "a Geminian" or "a Sagittarian", so each of the other planets occupied a certain sign. Each planet governs a different area of your personality, and the planets Venus and Mars are responsible for your attitudes to love and sex respectively.

For example, if you are a Sun-sign Sagittarian, according to the attributes of the sign you should be a dynamic, freedom-loving character. However, if Venus occupied Libra when you were born, you may make rather a passive and clinging partner – qualities that are supposedly completely alien to Sagittarians.

A MAP OF THE CONSTELLATION

The 16th-century astronomer Copernicus first made the revolutionary suggestion that the planets orbit the Sun rather than the Earth. In this 17th-century constellation chart, the Sun is shown at the centre of the solar system.

The tables on pages 52–61 of this book will enable you to discover the positions of Mars and Venus at the moment of your birth. Once you have gleaned this information, turn to pages 22–45. On these pages we explain how the influences of

Venus and Mars interact with the characteristics of your Sun sign. This information will provide you with many illuminating insights into your personality, and explains how the planets have formed your attitudes to love and sex.

LOOKING FOR A LOVER

ASTROLOGY CAN PROVIDE YOU WITH VALUABLE INFORMATION
ON HOW TO INITIATE AND MAINTAIN RELATIONSHIPS. IT CAN
ALSO TELL YOU HOW COMPATIBLE YOU ARE WITH YOUR LOVER,
AND HOW SUCCESSFUL YOUR RELATIONSHIP IS LIKELY TO BE.

*P*eople frequently use astrology to lead into a relationship, and "What sign are you?" is often used as a conversation opener. Some people simply introduce the subject as an opening gambit, while others place great importance on this question and its answer.

Astrology can affect the way you think and behave when you are in love. It can also provide you with fascinating information about your lovers and your relationships. Astrology cannot tell you who to fall in love with, or who to avoid, but it can offer you some very helpful advice.

BIRTH CHARTS
Synastry involves the comparison of two people's charts in order to assess their compatibility in all areas of their relationship. The process can highlight any areas of common interest or potential conflict.

THE TABLE OF ELEMENTS

People whose signs are grouped under the same element tend to find it easy to fall into a happy relationship. The groupings are:

FIRE: *Aries, Leo, Sagittarius*
EARTH: *Taurus, Virgo, Capricorn*
AIR: *Gemini, Libra, Aquarius*
WATER: *Cancer, Scorpio, Pisces*

When you meet someone to whom you are attracted, astrology can provide you with a valuable insight into his or her personality. It may even reveal unattractive characteristics that your prospective partner is trying to conceal.

Astrologers are often asked to advise lovers involved in an ongoing relationship, or people who are contemplating a love affair. This important aspect of astrology is called synastry, and involves comparing the birth charts of the two people concerned. Each birth chart records the exact position of the planets at the moment and place of a person's birth.

By interpreting each chart separately, then comparing them, an astrologer can assess the compatibility of any two people, showing where problems may arise in their relationship, and where strong bonds will form.

One of the greatest astrological myths is that people of some signs are not compatible with people of certain other signs. This is completely untrue. Whatever your Sun sign, you can have a happy relationship with a person of any other sign.

YOU & YOUR LOVER

KNOWING ABOUT YOURSELF AND YOUR LOVER IS THE KEY TO
A HAPPY RELATIONSHIP. HERE WE REVEAL THE TRADITIONAL
ASSOCIATIONS OF PISCES, YOUR COMPATIBILITY WITH ALL THE
SUN SIGNS, AND THE FLOWERS LINKED WITH EACH SIGN.

ALL TREES THAT GROW
NEAR WATER, SUCH AS
THE WILLOW, ARE
TRADITIONALLY
ASSOCIATED
WITH PISCES

THE COLOUR
ASSOCIATED
WITH PISCES
IS A MUTED
SEA-GREEN

PISCEANS HAVE
COMPACT, WELL-
BUILT BODIES,
BUT MAY HAVE
TO WORK HARD
TO CONTROL
THEIR WEIGHT

THE PLANET
NEPTUNE,
WHICH HAS
THE NAME OF
THE ROMAN
GOD OF THE
SEA, RULES
PISCES

ALL FISH ARE
RULED BY PISCES,
AS ARE ANY
MAMMALS THAT
LIVE IN OR
NEAR THE
WATER

AS PISCES IS A WATER
SIGN, THE MAJORITY
OF PISCEANS LIKE TO
LIVE NEAR WATER

PISCES AND ARIES

The lively vigour of Aries may intimidate a dreamy Piscean. However, if you use your gentle charms to calm a fiery Arien, this combination could lead to a contented and rewarding union.

Lavender is a Geminian flower

Thistles are ruled by Aries

PISCES AND GEMINI

A restless Geminian may seem heartless to an emotional Piscean. Flighty Geminians can even indulge in infidelity. Both of you must moderate your behaviour if your alliance is to succeed.

PISCES AND TAURUS

The warm passions of Taurus will boost your confidence, and your romantic charms will bring out the Taurean protective streak. This match is guaranteed to bring out the best in both of you.

The lily, and other white flowers, are ruled by Cancer

The rose is associated with Taurus

PISCES AND CANCER

You are both emotional water signs and are very compatible. This relationship will possess an aura of dreamy romance, and the two of you should enjoy a blissfully happy relationship.

PISCES AND LEO

Although you are very different creatures, you are both romantic daydreamers with a creative streak. You are quite happy for Leo to be the centre of attention, so there will be no clash of egos.

Hydrangeas are governed by Libra

PISCES AND LIBRA

Libra, like Pisces, is a romantic and considerate sign, and you will both try very hard to make and keep each other happy. This will be a supportive, loving, and sympathetic union.

Sunflowers are ruled by Leo

PISCES AND VIRGO

Virgo and Pisces are opposite signs of the zodiac, and are very compatible. Virgoans will keep you happy and secure, and you will delight them with your sense of poetry and romance.

Honeysuckle is attributed to Scorpio

PISCES AND SCORPIO

A gentle, dreamy Piscean could be intimidated by the intensity and power of Scorpio passion. Try to stand up for yourself and assert your personality, or a Scorpio may walk all over you.

Small, brightly-coloured flowers are associated with Virgo

PISCES AND SAGITTARIUS

If you become too overemotional, a carefree, footloose Sagittarian will simply gallop off into the distance and abandon you. Sagittarian optimism and good cheer will liven you up a little.

Orchids are associated with Aquarius

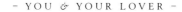

Carnations are ruled by Sagittarius

PISCES AND AQUARIUS

Your Piscean emotions may overwhelm a freedom-loving Aquarian. If you can understand that they need their own space, this has the potential to be a very loving and fulfilling match.

PISCES AND CAPRICORN

The will to succeed drives Capricornians, and their determination to win will not appeal to you. However, their reliability and solidity should make you feel very secure.

Viburnum is governed by Pisces

Pansies are Capricornian flowers

PISCES AND PISCES

Pisceans need a decisive and determined partner to help them reach their full potential. To make this match work, the pair of you must learn to be a little more organized and assertive.

THE FOOD OF LOVE

WHEN PLANNING A SEDUCTION, THE SENSUOUS DELIGHTS OF AN
EXQUISITE MEAL SHOULD NEVER BE UNDERESTIMATED. READ ON
TO DISCOVER THE PERFECT MEAL FOR EACH OF THE SUN SIGNS,
GUARANTEED TO AROUSE INTEREST AND STIR DESIRE.

*Pisceans will
find the subtle
and delicate flavour
of melon sorbet
particularly
appetizing.*

– THE FOOD OF LOVE –

FOR ARIENS

Spicy mulligatawny soup

·

Peppered steak

·

Baked Alaska

FOR TAUREANS

Cream of cauliflower soup

·

Tournedos Rossini

·

Rich chocolate and brandy mousse

FOR GEMINIANS

Seafood and avocado salad

·

Piquant stir-fried pork with ginger

·

Zabaglione

FOR CANCERIANS

Artichoke vinaigrette

·

Sole Bonne Femme

·

Almond soufflé

THE FOOD OF LOVE

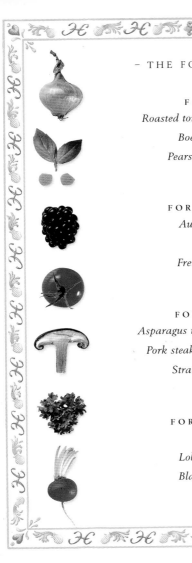

FOR LEOS

Roasted tomato and garlic soup
·
Boeuf Stroganoff
·
Pears cooked in wine

FOR VIRGOANS

Aubergine salad
·
Paella
·
French apple tart

FOR LIBRANS

Asparagus with hollandaise sauce
·
Pork steak with roasted apples
·
Strawberry Pavlova

FOR SCORPIOS

Vichyssoise
·
Lobster Newburg
·
Blackcurrant fool

- THE FOOD OF LOVE -

FOR SAGITTARIANS
Chilled cucumber soup
·
Nutty onion flan
·
Rhubarb crumble with fresh cream

FOR CAPRICORNIANS
Eggs Florentine
·
Pork tenderloin stuffed with sage
·
Pineapple Pavlova

FOR AQUARIANS
Watercress soup
·
Chicken cooked with chilli and lime
·
Lemon soufflé

FOR PISCEANS
French onion soup
·
Trout au vin rosé
·
Melon sorbet

PLACES TO LOVE

ONCE YOU HAVE WON YOUR LOVER'S HEART, A ROMANTIC
HOLIDAY TOGETHER WILL SET THE SEAL ON YOUR LOVE.
HERE YOU CAN DISCOVER THE PERFECT DESTINATION FOR EACH
SUN SIGN, FROM HISTORIC CITIES TO IDYLLIC BEACHES.

THE
EIFFEL
TOWER,
PARIS

ARIES

*Florence is an Arien
city, and its perfectly
preserved Renaissance
palaces and churches
will set the scene for
wonderful romance.*

TAURUS

*The unspoilt scenery
and unhurried pace
of life in rural Ireland
is sure to appeal to
patient and placid
Taureans.*

GEMINI

*Vivacious and restless
Geminians will feel at
home in the fast-paced
and sophisticated
atmosphere of
New York.*

CANCER

*The watery beauty
and uniquely romantic
atmosphere of Venice
is guaranteed to arouse
passion and stir the
Cancerian imagination.*

ST. BASIL'S
CATHEDRAL,
MOSCOW

AYERS ROCK/ULURU,
AUSTRALIA

LEO

Leos will fall in love all over again when surrounded by the picturesque charm and unspoilt medieval atmosphere of Prague.

VIRGO

Perhaps the most elegant and romantic of all cities, Paris is certainly the ideal setting for a stylish and fastidious Virgoan.

LIBRA

The dramatic and exotic beauty of Upper Egypt and the Nile will provide the perfect backdrop for wooing a romantic Libran.

SCORPIO

Intense and passionate Scorpios will be strongly attracted by the whiff of danger present in the exotic atmosphere of New Orleans.

SAGITTARIUS

The wide-ranging spaces of the Australian outback will appeal to the Sagittarian love of freedom and the great outdoors.

CAPRICORN

Capricornians will be fascinated and inspired by the great historical monuments of Moscow, the most powerful of all Russian cities.

AQUARIUS

Intrepid Aquarians will be enthralled and amazed by the unusual sights and spectacular landscapes of the Indian subcontinent.

PISCES

Water-loving Pisceans will be at their most relaxed and romantic by the sea, perhaps on a small and unspoilt Mediterranean island.

THE PYRAMIDS, EGYPT

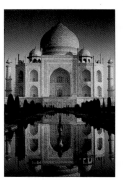

GONDOLAS, VENICE

THE TAJ MAHAL, INDIA

VENUS & MARS

LUCID, SHINING VENUS AND FIERY, RED MARS HAVE ALWAYS
BEEN ASSOCIATED WITH HUMAN LOVE AND PASSION. THE TWO
PLANETS HAVE A POWERFUL INFLUENCE ON OUR ATTITUDES
TOWARDS LOVE, SEX, AND RELATIONSHIPS.

The study of astrology first began long before humankind began to record its own history. The earliest astrological artefacts discovered, scratches on bones recording the phases of the Moon, date from well before the invention of any alphabet or writing system.

The planets Venus and Mars have always been regarded as having enormous significance in astrology. This is evident from the tentative attempts of early astrologers to record the effects of the two planets on humankind. Hundreds of years later, the positions of the planets were carefully noted in personal horoscopes. The earliest known record is dated 410 BC: "Venus [was] in the Bull, and Mars in the Twins".

The bright, shining planet Venus represents the gentle effect of the soul on our physical lives. It is responsible for a refined and romantic sensuality – "pure" love, untainted by sex. Venus reigns over our attitudes towards romance and the spiritual dimension of love.

The planet Mars affects the physical aspects of our lives – our strength, both physical and mental; our endurance; and our ability to fight for survival. Mars is also strongly linked to the sex drive of both men and women. Mars governs our physical energy, sexuality, and levels of desire.

Venus is known as an "inferior" planet, because its orbit falls between Earth and the Sun. Venus orbits the Sun

LOVE CONQUERS ALL
In Botticelli's Venus and Mars, *the warlike, fiery
energy of Mars, the god of war, has been overcome by
the gentle charms of Venus, the goddess of love.*

closely, and its position in the zodiac is always in a sign near that of the Sun. As a result, the planet can only have occupied one of five given signs at the time of your birth – your Sun sign, or the two signs before or after it. For example, if you were born with the Sun in Virgo, Venus can only have occupied Cancer, Leo, Virgo, Libra, or Scorpio at that moment.

Mars, on the other hand, is a "superior" planet. Its orbit lies on the other side of the Earth from the Sun, and therefore the planet may have occupied any of the 12 signs at the moment of your birth.

On the following pages (24–45) we provide you with fascinating insights into how Mars and Venus govern your attitudes towards love, sex, and relationships. To ascertain which sign of the zodiac the planets occupied at the moment of your birth, you must first consult the tables on pages 52–61. Then turn to page 24 and read on.

YOUR LOVE LIFE

THE PLANET VENUS REPRESENTS LOVE, HARMONY, AND UNISON.
WORK OUT WHICH SIGN OF THE ZODIAC VENUS OCCUPIED AT
THE MOMENT OF YOUR BIRTH (SEE PAGES 52–57), AND READ ON.

VENUS IN CAPRICORN

*F*rom Capricorn, Venus will help to curb the powerful waves of Piscean passion that continually wash over you. When you fall in love, this restraining influence will prove extremely beneficial. Venus in Capricorn will not lessen your ability to have fun, or make you less affectionate, but it will bring a practical aspect to your personality that your fellow Pisceans may envy.

From this sign, Venus will play the part of a gentle yet practical friend, bringing you a strong streak of Capricornian caution and common sense. Your powerful and changeable emotions will be easier to control, and you are less likely to pledge yourself forever

on the basis of a brief spark of attraction. Instead, you will choose your lover very carefully and thoughtfully.

When Venus shines from Capricorn, material status will be very important to you. When you look around for a potential long-term partner, you may choose someone for the wrong reasons – perhaps because he or she is particularly attractive, intelligent, or wealthy. You may regard your lover as a trophy that you have won, exciting envy and admiration in others. Do not allow worldly ambition to persuade you to pick a lover for the wrong reasons – such a partnership will not be built on a solid foundation and is unlikely to enjoy lasting success.

Venus in Capricorn emphasizes duty and diligence, and you will work hard for your family. You enjoy the role of provider, and will want your family life to be secure both financially and emotionally. As a result, you may gradually find yourself working longer and longer hours, and reducing the amount of time you can spend with your partner and family. Do not neglect your domestic life. Try to spend your time as sensibly as you spend your money, and divide your time and energy equally between your work and your home life.

All Pisceans have a generous amount of love and affection to lavish on their fortunate partner, and you have the ability to combine that love with a valuable element of common sense. As a result, you will make a warm-hearted, passionate, and supportive partner.

VENUS IN AQUARIUS

*W*hen Venus shines from Aquarius, the planet will imbue you with an enigmatic allure and an indefinable air of glamour. You are likely to be surrounded by a throng of admirers, and will revel in the attention they lavish upon you.

Although you will enjoy all this admiration and attention, due to the independent, freedom-loving influence of Aquarius you may be somewhat apprehensive when a friend or lover indicates a desire to move your relationship on to a more serious level. When Venus occupies Aquarius, you will be essentially a free spirit, and if asked to make a long-term commitment you may experience an uncharacteristic urge to beat a hasty retreat, or even slump into a depression as you realize just how much your privacy and independence will be curtailed by a permanent partnership. In such a

situation, you must draw on all your Piscean romanticism and tenderness, and fight off any Aquarian reluctance to make a serious commitment.

The cool restraint brought by Venus in Aquarius will be most helpful, because it will help you to regulate the intensity and passion of your Piscean emotions. You will find it easier to control your powerful feelings and to assume a more rational outlook on life. The Aquarian influence will also bring you a valuable infusion of practical common sense, combined with a keen sense of intuition.

People born under this planetary placing tend to be attracted by lovely things and beautiful people. Appearances can sometimes assume too much importance for you. It is not wise to select a partner on the basis of looks alone – your relationship must be built on sturdier foundations. Friendship and understanding will endure forever, whereas the appeal of beauty will eventually fade.

Due to the kindness of Pisces and the loyalty of Aquarius, you will be a faithful and constant friend, always ready to supply moral support and to provide a sympathetic ear. However, Pisceans often have a perverse streak and you may find that you can be contrary when it comes to fitting in with the wishes of others. Despite this trait, your kindness and generosity will ensure that you are a popular and valued companion.

The combination of your innate Piscean tenderness and romance and your Aquarian sparkle and glamour is irresistible. Due to this planetary placing, you are guaranteed to be an extremely sought-after and seductive lover.

VENUS IN PISCES

*A*ccording to astrological tradition, Venus is very harmoniously and happily placed in Pisces. However, when both the Sun and Venus occupy this sign, the powerful influence of Pisces will need careful control.

Pisceans tend to fall in love very easily. You are extremely trusting and open-hearted, and almost anyone who sets out to win you over will easily succeed. You should be aware that your abundance of Piscean emotions may quite unexpectedly run away with you. As a result, you may find yourself making rash and generous sacrifices for your partner. Pisceans have an inclination to idolize their lovers, and tend to regard them in the flattering glow of rose-coloured spectacles. You may even treat your partner in such a devoted and adoring fashion that he or she begins to take you for granted and eventually treats you like a doormat. If your partner turns out to be selfish or inconsiderate, there is a danger that your kind-hearted and altruistic nature might be ruthlessly exploited.

Pisceans are so idealistic when it comes to affairs of the heart that they do not always learn by their mistakes. If you manage to extricate yourself from an unhappy relationship or a self-obsessed and uncaring lover, you are likely to fall head over heels in love two weeks later, and may be well on the way to experiencing the same heartbreak all over again. You must strive to adopt a more cautious and judicious attitude when searching for a lover. Before committing yourself, you must consider how compatible you and your potential partner are, and once you are involved keep a sharp eye open for any flaws in his or her character.

Dreamy, poetic Pisceans have an amazing ability to avoid facing facts, which can be very difficult if their relationships enter into troubled waters. You have a tendency to take the easy way out of emotional upsets by pretending that nothing is wrong, which is not a very constructive solution to problems within your relationship. Try to cultivate a little less emotion and a little more common sense.

Pisceans can sometimes bowl over a potential partner with their ardour and romanticism. When you meet someone you are attracted to, you must not feel rebuffed if he or she is not quite as responsive and enthusiastic as you, because not everybody is so open with their feelings. From Venus, Pisces can bring a tendency towards self-doubt. Do not underestimate your powers of attraction.

VENUS IN ARIES

*T*he watery and sensitive emotions of Pisces will be transformed by the fiery and ardent influence of Venus in Aries. You will be caring and tender, but at the same time vigorous and enthusiastic. However, your powerful Piscean emotions will still dominate your personality and will gush out in a torrent when you meet someone you find attractive.

You may discover that Arien determination and forcefulness clash with your Piscean lack of confidence. Due to the bold and impetuous influence of Venus in Aries, when you are attracted to someone your instinct will be to pursue him or her openly and eagerly. However, an element of Piscean self-doubt could dampen down your eagerness and enthusiasm, and you may be reluctant to make your feelings obvious. Employ all your Arien dynamism and courage to overcome any insecurities, and allow the warm and enthusiastic aspects of your personality to come to the fore.

With this placing, Piscean romanticism is likely to combine with Arien impetuosity, and when you fall in love, you will regard each new liaison as the great passion of your life, throwing yourself headlong into the relationship. This may not always be the wisest approach to adopt, because if your alliance does not succeed you will be disillusioned and saddened. Try not to be too impulsive and reckless – instead try to cultivate the valuable qualities of caution and prudence.

You will be a generous partner, happy to lavish both money and emotion on your partner. Generosity is highly attractive, but your open-handed attitude to money may lead you into financial difficulties.

Pisceans tend to be easy-going and compliant, happy to fall in with the wishes of their friends and lovers. However, when Venus shines from Aries, a most uncharacteristic streak of selfishness could manifest itself in your personality. A ruthless determination to always get your own way is not an attractive attribute, therefore keep a sharp look-out for any self-indulgence and self-absorption.

The gentle and considerate Piscean elements in your personality should help you to quash any selfish urges.

If you are able to combine the valuable strength and energy of Venus in Aries with your innate Piscean gentleness and sensuality, you will make a considerate yet dynamic partner, and will find it easy to form an extremely happy, long-lasting, and successful relationship.

VENUS IN TAURUS

*I*n astrological terms, Venus "rules" Taurus, and therefore the planet will work very powerfully for you. From Taurus, the influence of Venus is loving and tender, and you will do everything in your power to keep your lover contented and fulfilled. As a lover, you will be extremely generous and altruistic, and will lavish attention on your fortunate partner.

Pisceans are often extremely emotional types, and when they fall for someone, they fall head over heels, and without restraint. This recklessness can lead to heartbreak and disillusionment. Luckily, from Taurus, Venus will provide a more cautious and level-headed influence. You are less likely than many Pisceans to throw yourself fervently into an affair, and will be quite happy to approach a new relationship slowly and steadily, feeling that there is no need to rush.

Pisceans are intensely romantic, and you will revel in the heady atmosphere of romance and excitement that pervades the early stages of a relationship. Your courtship and seduction will be characterized by luxury, for you are likely to have a true Taurean appreciation of the good things in life – delicious food, fine wines, and comfortable and elegant surroundings. Venus in Taurus often brings with it a love of rich food, therefore you may have to struggle to keep your weight down.

From Taurus, the influence of Venus could make you rather possessive – a trait that your partner may find difficult to tolerate. Fortunately, Venus will make you more practical and emotionally stable than some Pisceans, and will bring you a generous helping of common sense. This should enable you to recognize any pangs of possessiveness and firmly quell them. Do not fall into the trap of thinking of your lover as belonging to you, as if he or she were a beautiful but inanimate object.

Should things go wrong between you and your partner, there is a possibility that you may feel bitter and mean-spirited. As a result you may strive to hurt your lover in any way possible. Deep down, you are all too aware that revenge is a negative emotion that will not mend your broken heart, and therefore you must try to remain rational in such circumstances.

You will find that Venus in Taurus gives you the enviable ability to achieve both financial and emotional stability – Venus will bring you considerable common sense, and a loving but eminently practical attitude to both love and money.

YOUR SEX LIFE

THE PLANET MARS REPRESENTS PHYSICAL AND SEXUAL ENERGY.
WORK OUT WHICH SIGN OF THE ZODIAC MARS OCCUPIED AT THE
MOMENT OF YOUR BIRTH (SEE PAGES 58–61), AND READ ON.

MARS IN ARIES

When Mars shines from Aries, you will possess a high level of physical energy, which will increase both your sex drive and your level of emotional passion.

You will be an ardent and rewarding lover, because the fiery passion of Aries will complement the romantic ardour of the typical Piscean. Arien energy and enthusiasm will overcome any Piscean lack of confidence, and you will be more assertive than many of your fellow Pisceans.

Any Piscean propensity to self-deception will be lessened by Mars in Aries, and you will be a forthright and honest lover, scorning deceit and insincerity.

MARS IN TAURUS

*F*rom Taurus, Mars will bring you a degree of sexual passion that will rival your Piscean emotional resources in its intensity. As a result, you will be an extremely sensual and affectionate lover.

Due to the influence of Taurus, you will have greater physical stamina than many Pisceans, spiced with a touch of stubbornness. Taurean tenacity will make you very determined – once you have set your heart on something you will do your utmost to achieve it. This applies to potential lovers as well as ambitions or material possessions.

The Taurean influence is usually a placid one, and this placing should have a steadying effect on your volatile emotions. When upset, Pisceans are more likely to burst into tears than to throw plates, but you may possess a hot temper. This will lie dormant for much of the time but, when your anger flares up, the resulting scene will be an extremely stormy one.

MARS IN GEMINI

*T*his placing of Mars will heighten your sexual appetite. You will throw yourself with enthusiasm into the sexual side of your relationship, and will be eager to experiment. The adventurous Geminian attitude to sex will combine with Piscean passion and eroticism, and as a result, your lovemaking will be seductive and imaginative.

When Mars is in Gemini, you will thrive on novelty and change. Gemini is the sign of duality, and Pisceans tend to be a trifle deceptive. Resist the temptation to become involved in illicit affairs. You must not allow a yearning for excitement to endanger a happy and secure relationship. Luckily, you will find it easy to discuss any problems with your partner, as you are likely to be articulate and eloquent.

You will be a vigorous and athletic lover with plenty of stamina and, of all the Sun signs, are most likely to remain sexually active well into old age.

MARS IN CANCER

$\mathscr{P}$isceans are renowned for their tender and romantic approach to love, and the influence of Cancer will make you even more sensual and caring. Your lovemaking will be passionate yet tender, and you will be an extremely seductive and imaginative lover.

You will have an instinctive awareness of your partner's needs and desires, and will work hard to ensure that he or she is satisfied and fulfilled. There is a danger that you could be almost too devoted, making your lover feel claustrophobic. Bear in mind the force of your emotions – if they are intently focused on your lover, your feelings could be overwhelming in their intensity.

Pisceans are usually sweet-natured and easy-going, but from Cancer Mars may make you a little touchy. In the heat of an argument, you may make hurtful comments. Try to control your sharp tongue, or you could find that it makes mischief between you and your lover.

MARS IN LEO

*F*rom Leo, Mars will bring you a great zest for life, coupled with a determination that your friends and lover should enjoy themselves as much as you. This concern for the happiness of others extends to your sex life, and ensures that you will be a considerate and generous lover.

The influence of Mars from Leo will make you a natural leader – resourceful, determined, and energetic. Leonine vitality and dynamism will soon overcome any Piscean lack of confidence or self-doubt. When you meet a potential partner you will pursue your quarry forcefully and boldly, and will employ all the seductive charm Mars brings from Leo to win the heart of your prospective lover.

You have a hot temper which tends to flare up suddenly and unexpectedly. Try to resist the temptation to cause a scene. Happily, your anger will die down as quickly as it bubbles up, and you will soon be eager to kiss and make up with your lover.

MARS IN VIRGO

*T*he uncontrolled torrent of Piscean emotion may be checked by the cool influence of Mars from Virgo, but do not allow the sign to repress your warm Piscean sensuality. If you can allow the passion of Pisces to develop the earthy sensuality of Virgo, you will be a rewarding and passionate lover.

Pisceans tend to be very impulsive, throwing themselves into relationships without a great deal of forethought. If their alliance does not succeed, they often become disillusioned and depressed. However, Mars in Virgo will provide a cautious and practical influence. You will be more self-controlled when it comes to forming relationships, and less likely to fling yourself into a disastrous liaison.

You are a dutiful and hard-working lover, and will labour with all the Virgoan diligence and Piscean emotional energy you possess to ensure that your relationship is fulfilling, harmonious, and long-lasting.

MARS IN LIBRA

*W*hen Mars shines from Libra, you will want to enjoy a passionate and sensuous sex life within the secure confines of a harmonious and long-lasting relationship. Due to the Libran influence, you may be a little languid, and the prospect of energetic sex will not always appeal. You must overcome your laziness, because once aroused you are an ardent, skilful lover.

You will work hard to achieve a happy and sexually fulfilling relationship, but do not become ingratiating in your attempts to keep your lover content. There is a danger that such an attitude may become cloying and claustrophobic.

Although Libra tends to dampen down the energy of Mars, the planet may encourage you to argue with your lover. The Libran influence is generally a peaceful one, but when it comes to romantic relationships, you may cause quarrels simply because you so enjoy the ritual of kissing and making up.

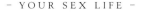

MARS IN SCORPIO

*F*rom Scorpio, the Martian influence is extremely powerful, and will increase your sex drive. As a result, your love-making will be passionate and erotically charged.

As a result, it is essential that you find a partner who possesses a similarly high libido. A romantic and sensual sex life is important to all Pisceans, but due to the influence of Scorpio you may become very frustrated and irritable if you do not enjoy frequent and satisfying sex.

Pisceans tend to be gentle and considerate lovers, but when Mars shines from Scorpio, you may find that jealousy rears its ugly head. You may become possessive, filled with a black rage if your partner pays any attention to someone else. As your emotions are strong, any jealousy will be very evident, and could create an oppressive atmosphere within your relationship. You must draw on all your Piscean kindness and sensitivity to overcome this destructive emotion.

– YOUR SEX LIFE –

MARS IN SAGITTARIUS

When Mars shines from Sagittarius, the planet will fill you with energy and zest for life. You will be more active and adventurous than many Pisceans, and as a result, your sex life will be dynamic, imaginative, and exciting.

This planetary placing suggests that you will thrive on constant challenge and novelty, and a partner who can stimulate your mind and equal your sex drive will be a perfect match for you. If you are not mentally and physically fulfilled by your partner, you may become restless and could even turn to illicit affairs to provide a spark of excitement.

Pisceans tend to be very selfless and happy to comply with the wishes of others. However, the Sagittarian influence will make you more assertive and less malleable. This is a beneficial influence, because it should prevent you from adopting a submissive role within your relationship.

MARS IN CAPRICORN

*T*he placing of Mars in Capricorn can be very beneficial for a Piscean. The cool and restrained Capricornian influence will steady your rather volatile emotions and impart a valuable degree of self-control and discipline.

When Mars shines from Capricorn, you are unlikely to be an uncontrollably passionate lover. However, you will possess a consistently strong sex drive and plenty of stamina. Capricornians aim to excel at everything they turn their hands to, therefore when Mars occupies this sign your lovemaking will be skilled and expert.

Due to the Capricornian influence from Mars, you will be ambitious and determined. Once you have set your sights on a potential lover, you will not rest until you have won his or her heart. A degree of Capricornian forcefulness and determination will make a valuable addition to your easy-going Piscean personality.

MARS IN AQUARIUS

*F*rom Aquarius, Mars may lessen the strength of your emotions. This will only work to your advantage, because your powerful Piscean feelings can so easily run away with you. You will possess more self-control than the majority of Pisceans and will be less likely to burst into tears or throw a tantrum.

Aquarius tends to bring a rather remote and detached influence from Mars, but despite this you will still possess a strong and steady sex drive. Pisceans are passionate and imaginative lovers, and your sex life will be active and inventive.

Mars in Aquarius will bring you a love of independence, and you will demand a degree of freedom within your relationship. This placing is likely to bring you a decidedly unconventional streak, and you may find that you are stubbornly determined to have your own way. Try not to become too eccentric, or potential suitors may be intimidated by your unorthodox behaviour.

MARS IN PISCES

*W*hen Mars occupies Pisces with the Sun, your powerful emotions will be increased. Your physical energy may not be very enduring, but you will be an imaginative, passionate, and sensual lover.

Pisceans are extremely tender-hearted and romantic, and when you fall in love, there is a danger that you may over-whelm your new lover with the force of your emotions. You must try not to overpower your partner with passionate demonstrations of your love, for your constant attentions may create a claustrophobic and restrictive atmosphere.

When the Sun and Mars both shine from Pisces, you will be an idealistic and starry-eyed lover. You are likely to possess the typical Piscean tendency to place your lover on a pedestal. Try not to adulate him or her too much, because you will be sorely disappointed when you eventually realize that your idol has feet of clay.

TOKENS OF LOVE

ASTROLOGY CAN GIVE YOU A FASCINATING INSIGHT INTO
YOUR LOVER'S PERSONALITY AND ATTITUDE TO LOVE. IT CAN
ALSO PROVIDE YOU WITH SOME INVALUABLE HINTS WHEN
YOU WANT TO CHOOSE THE PERFECT GIFT FOR YOUR LOVER.

INDIAN
HAIR
ORNAMENT

BELGIAN
CHOCOLATES

ARIES
The head is the part
of the body ruled by
Aries, and unusual
hair products or
accessories
will make
an ideal
present.

TAPESTRY
CUSHION

TAURUS
A lavish and luxurious
cushion will enchant your
Taurean lover, as will rich
hand-made chocolates.

GEMINI
Instead of chocolates,
buy your Geminian
lover sugared almonds
or mixed nuts.

SUGARED
ALMONDS

BRASS BIRD
CURIO

CANCER

*Cancerians adore unusual
curios and will also be
delighted by luxurious soap.
The pearl is the Cancerian
gemstone, and pearl jewellery
will be a meaningful gift.*

DELICATELY-
SCENTED
SOAP

LEO

*Flamboyant Leos appreciate
boldly-coloured, hand-
crafted objects. Gold is the
Leo metal, and anything
gold or golden-coloured
will have great appeal.*

CRAFTWORK
BROOCH

PEARL
NECKLACE

GOLD
'COCKTAIL'
WRISTWATCH

REGENCY-
STYLE
WOODEN
CHAIR

VIRGO

*Any objects made
from wood will
make the perfect
gift for Virgoans,
because they are
drawn to natural
materials.*

– TOKENS OF LOVE –

WHITE
ROSES

LIBRA
*Romantic Librans will
revel in seductive gifts
such as bouquets of
roses or silky lingerie.*

SILK
LINGERIE

TABLE
LAMP

SCORPIO
*A handsome lamp
is sure to occupy
pride of place in
a Scorpio home.*

SAGITTARIUS
*Adventurous Sagittarians
love to travel, and travel
books and accessories, such
as maps or compasses, will
be greatly appreciated.*

TRAVEL
BOOKS

VICTORIAN
COMPASS

- TOKENS OF LOVE -

CAPRICORN

An old-fashioned fountain pen, elegant candles, or a glass decanter will all impress a fastidious Capricornian.

FOUNTAIN PEN

HEART-PATTERNED CANDLES

HAND-BLOWN GLASS

GIVING A BIRTHSTONE

The most personal gift you can give your lover is the gem linked to his or her Sun sign.

MOONSTONE

ARIES: *diamond*
TAURUS: *emerald*
GEMINI: *agate* • CANCER: *pearl*
LEO: *ruby* • VIRGO: *sardonyx*
LIBRA: *sapphire* • SCORPIO: *opal*
SAGITTARIUS: *topaz*
CAPRICORN: *amethyst*
AQUARIUS: *aquamarine*
PISCES: *moonstone*

WHITE ORCHID

AQUARIUS

Aquarians adore unusual and original gifts, such as hand-made modern glassware. If you are giving your Aquarian lover flowers, choose orchids.

PISCES

A sumptuous silk scarf will beguile a sensual Piscean. Iridescent glassware will also delight your Piscean lover.

THAI SILK SCARF

YOUR PERMANENT RELATIONSHIP

PISCEANS POUR THEIR PLENTIFUL SUPPLIES OF EMOTION INTO
THEIR PERMANENT RELATIONSHIPS. ROMANTIC AND SENTIMENTAL,
YOU WILL WORK HARD TO ACHIEVE A SUCCESSFUL PARTNERSHIP.

Tenderness and affection are the trademarks of a Piscean in love, and you will make a sympathetic and caring partner. You are prepared to work hard to ensure that your relationship is successful, happy, and long-lasting.

Pisceans have an unfortunate tendency to adopt a rather submissive role within their relationships – make sure that you do not repress your own wishes and opinions. Your submission could encourage your partner to become selfish, and you could find yourself always giving way to him or her. Such adoring submission might initially be flattering, but your partner could eventually feel overwhelmed by your dependency. It is important that you retain a sense of your own identity and voice your own opinions, rather than always deferring to your partner.

Pisceans often have a high emotional level, which you should try to keep under control. This does not mean that you cannot occasionally allow your emotions free rein, but a continual storm of emotion can lead to needless confrontations. Pisceans can worry unduly about their lovers, largely because of their fertile imaginations. You may think that things are going horribly wrong with your relationship, when in fact all is entirely harmonious. Try to keep a logical perspective. Do not let your vivid imagination

A JOINT FUTURE
On a Sailing Ship, *by Caspar David Friedrich, shows a newly-married couple sailing into a bright but unknown future together.*

run away with you – any unpunctuality on the part of your lover is far more likely to be due to heavy traffic than to any great disaster or catastrophe.

If problems arise in your relationship, resist the typical Piscean habit of trying to wriggle out of accepting the blame. This behaviour may worsen the situation. Try to own up to your misdemeanours rather than making excuses.

Pisceans hate to hurt others, and can economize with the truth in order to extricate themselves from a difficult situation, or to avoid hurting their lover's feelings. Resist the temptation to be evasive or vague. Talk any problems through – the ability to discuss your altercations honestly is one of the major ingredients of a successful relationship.

VENUS & MARS TABLES

THESE TABLES WILL ENABLE YOU TO DISCOVER WHICH SIGNS
VENUS AND MARS OCCUPIED AT THE MOMENT OF YOUR BIRTH.
TURN TO PAGES 24–45 TO INVESTIGATE THE QUALITIES OF THESE
SIGNS, AND TO FIND OUT HOW THEY WORK WITH YOUR SUN SIGN.

*T*he tables on pages 53–61 will enable you to discover the positions of Venus and Mars at the moment of your birth.

First find your year of birth on the top line of the appropriate table, then find your month of birth in the left-hand column. Where the column for your year of birth intersects with the row for your month of birth, you will find a group of figures and zodiacal glyphs. These figures and glyphs show which sign of the zodiac the planet occupied

on the first day of that month, and any date during that month on which the planet moved into another sign.

For example, to ascertain the position of Venus on May 10 1968, run your finger down the column marked 1968 until you reach the row for May. The row of numbers and glyphs shows that Venus occupied Aries on May 1, entered Taurus on May 4, and then moved into Gemini on May 28. Therefore, on May 10, Venus was in Taurus.

If you were born on a day when one of the planets was moving into a new sign, it may be impossible to determine your Venus and Mars signs completely accurately. If the characteristics described on the relevant pages do not seem to apply to you, read the interpretation of the sign before and after. One of these signs will be appropriate.

ZODIACAL GLYPHS

♈	Aries	♎	Libra
♉	Taurus	♏	Scorpio
♊	Gemini	♐	Sagittarius
♋	Cancer	♑	Capricorn
♌	Leo	♒	Aquarius
♍	Virgo	♓	Pisces

– VENUS TABLES –

♀	1921	1922	1923	1924	1925	1926	1927	1928
JAN	1♒ 7♓	1♑ 25♒	1♏ 3♐	1♒ 20♓	1♐ 15♑	1♒	1♑ 10♒	1♏ 5♐ 30♑
FEB	1♓ 3♈	1♒ 18♓	1♐ 7♑	1♓ 14♈	1♑ 8♒	1♒	1♒ 3♓ 27♈	1♑ 23♒
MAR	1♈ 8♉	1♓ 14♈	1♑ 7♒	1♈ 10♉	1♒ 5♓ 29♈	1♒	1♈ 23♉	1♒ 19♓
APR	1♉ 26♈	1♈ 7♉	1♒ 2♓ 27♈	1♉ 8♊	1♈ 22♉	1♒ 7♓	1♉ 17♊	1♓ 12♈
MAY	1♈	1♉ 2♊ 26♋	1♈ 22♉	1♊ 7♋	1♉ 16♊	1♓ 7♈	1♊ 13♋	1♈ 7♉ 31♊
JUN	1♈ 3♉	1♋ 20♌	1♉ 16♊	1♋	1♊ 10♋	1♈ 3♉ 29♊	1♋ 9♌	1♊ 24♋
JUL	1♉ 9♊	1♌ 16♍	1♊ 11♋	1♋	1♋ 4♌ 29♍	1♊ 25♋	1♌ 8♍	1♋ 19♌
AUG	1♊ 6♋	1♍ 11♎	1♋ 4♌ 28♍	1♋	1♍ 23♎	1♋ 19♌	1♍	1♌ 12♍
SEP	1♌ 27♍	1♌ 8♍	1♍ 22♎	1♋ 8♌	1♎ 17♏	1♌ 19♍	1♍	1♍ 5♎ 30♏
OCT	1♍ 21♎	1♏ 11♐	1♎ 16♏	1♌ 8♍	1♏ 12♐	1♍ 6♎ 30♏	1♍	1♏ 24♐
NOV	1♎ 14♏	1♐ 29♏	1♏ 9♐	1♍ 3♎ 28♏	1♐ 7♑	1♏ 23♐	1♍ 10♎	1♐ 18♑
DEC	1♏ 8♐ 31♑	1♏	1♐ 3♑ 27♒	1♏ 22♐	1♑ 6♒	1♐ 17♑	1♎ 9♏	1♑ 13♒

♀	1929	1930	1931	1932	1933	1934	1935	1936
JAN	1♒ 7♓	1♑ 25♒	1♏ 4♐	1♒ 20♓	1♐ 15♑	1♒	1♑ 9♒	1♏ 4♐ 29♑
FEB	1♓ 3♈	1♒ 17♓	1♐ 7♑	1♓ 13♈	1♑ 8♒	1♒	1♒ 2♓ 27♈	1♑ 23♒
MAR	1♈ 9♉	1♓ 13♈	1♑ 6♒	1♈ 10♉	1♒ 4♓ 28♈	1♒	1♈ 23♉	1♒ 18♓
APR	1♉ 21♈	1♈ 7♉	1♓ 27♈	1♉ 6♊	1♈ 21♉	1♒ 7♓	1♉ 17♊	1♓ 12♈
MAY	1♈	1♉ 2♊ 26♋	1♈ 22♉	1♊ 7♋	1♉ 16♊	1♓ 7♈	1♊ 12♋	1♈ 6♉ 30♊
JUN	1♈ 4♉	1♋ 20♌	1♉ 15♊	1♋	1♊ 9♋	1♈ 3♉ 29♊	1♋ 8♌	1♊ 24♋
JUL	1♉ 9♊	1♌ 15♍	1♊ 10♋	1♋ 14♊ 29♋	1♋ 4♌ 28♍	1♊ 24♋	1♌ 8♍	1♋ 18♌
AUG	1♊ 6♋	1♍ 11♎	1♋ 4♌ 28♍	1♋	1♍ 22♎	1♋ 18♌	1♍	1♌ 12♍
SEP	1♌ 26♍	1♌ 8♍	1♍ 21♎	1♋ 9♌	1♎ 16♏	1♌ 12♍	1♍	1♍ 5♎ 29♏
OCT	1♍ 21♎	1♏ 13♐	1♎ 15♏	1♌ 8♍	1♏ 12♐	1♍ 6♎ 30♏	1♍	1♏ 24♐
NOV	1♎ 14♏	1♐ 23♏	1♏ 8♐	1♍ 3♎ 28♏	1♐ 7♑	1♏ 23♐	1♍ 8♎	1♐ 17♑
DEC	1♏ 8♐ 31♑	1♏	1♐ 2♑ 26♒	1♏ 22♐	1♑ 6♒	1♐ 17♑	1♎ 9♏	1♑ 12♒

♀	1937	1938	1939	1940	1941	1942	1943	1944
JAN	1 ♒ 7 ♓	1 ♑ 24 ♒	1 ♏ 5 ♐	1 ♒ 19 ♓	1 ♐ 14 ♑	1 ♒	1 ♑ 9 ♒	1 ♏ 4 ♐ 29 ♑
FEB	1 ♓ 3 ♈	1 ♒ 17 ♓	1 ♐ 7 ♑	1 ♓ 13 ♈	1 ♑ 7 ♒	1 ♒	1 ♒ 2 ♓ 26 ♈	1 ♑ 22 ♒
MAR	1 ♈ 10 ♉	1 ♓ 13 ♈	1 ♑ 6 ♒	1 ♈ 9 ♉	1 ♒ 3 ♓ 28 ♈	1 ♒	1 ♈ 22 ♉	1 ♒ 18 ♓
APR	1 ♉ 15 ♈	1 ♈ 6 ♉ 30 ♊	1 ♓ 5 ♈	1 ♉ 5 ♊	1 ♈ 21 ♉	1 ♒ 23 ♓	1 ♉ 16 ♊	1 ♓ 11 ♈
MAY	1 ♈	1 ♊ 25 ♋	1 ♈ 21 ♉	1 ♉ 7 ♊	1 ♉ 15 ♊	1 ♓ 7 ♈	1 ♊ 12 ♋	1 ♈ 5 ♉ 30 ♊
JUN	1 ♈ 5 ♉	1 ♋ 19 ♌	1 ♉ 15 ♊	1 ♋	1 ♊ 8 ♋	1 ♈ 3 ♉ 28 ♊	1 ♋ 8 ♌	1 ♊ 23 ♋
JUL	1 ♉ 8 ♊	1 ♌ 15 ♍	1 ♊ 10 ♋	1 ♋	1 ♋ 3 ♌ 28 ♍	1 ♋ 24 ♌	1 ♌ 8 ♍	1 ♋ 18 ♌
AUG	1 ♊ 5 ♋	1 ♍ 10 ♎	1 ♋ 3 ♌ 27 ♍	1 ♋ 2 ♌	1 ♍ 22 ♎	1 ♋ 18 ♌	1 ♍	1 ♌ 11 ♍
SEP	1 ♌ 26 ♍	1 ♎ 8 ♏	1 ♍ 21 ♎	1 ♋ 9 ♌	1 ♎ 16 ♏	1 ♌ 11 ♍	1 ♍	1 ♍ 4 ♎ 29 ♏
OCT	1 ♍ 20 ♎	1 ♏ 14 ♐	1 ♎ 15 ♏	1 ♌ 7 ♍	1 ♏ 11 ♐	1 ♍ 5 ♎ 29 ♏	1 ♍	1 ♏ 23 ♐
NOV	1 ♎ 13 ♏	1 ♐ 16 ♏	1 ♏ 8 ♐	1 ♍ 2 ♎ 27 ♏	1 ♐ 7 ♑	1 ♏ 22 ♐	1 ♎ 10 ♏	1 ♐ 17 ♑
DEC	1 ♏ 7 ♐ 31 ♑	1 ♏	1 ♐ 2 ♑ 26 ♒	1 ♏ 21 ♐	1 ♑ 6 ♒	1 ♐ 16 ♑	1 ♎ 9 ♏	1 ♑ 12 ♒

♀	1945	1946	1947	1948	1949	1950	1951	1952
JAN	1 ♒ 6 ♓	1 ♑ 23 ♒	1 ♏ 6 ♐	1 ♒ 19 ♓	1 ♐ 14 ♑	1 ♒	1 ♑ 8 ♒	1 ♏ 3 ♐ 28 ♑
FEB	1 ♓ 3 ♈	1 ♒ 16 ♓	1 ♐ 7 ♑	1 ♓ 12 ♈	1 ♑ 7 ♒	1 ♒	1 ♓ 25 ♈	1 ♑ 21 ♒
MAR	1 ♈ 12 ♉	1 ♓ 12 ♈	1 ♑ 6 ♒ 31 ♓	1 ♈ 9 ♉	1 ♒ 3 ♓ 27 ♈	1 ♒	1 ♈ 22 ♉	1 ♒ 17 ♓
APR	1 ♉ 8 ♈	1 ♈ 6 ♉ 30 ♊	1 ♓ 26 ♈	1 ♉ 5 ♊	1 ♈ 20 ♉	1 ♒ 7 ♓	1 ♉ 16 ♊	1 ♓ 10 ♈
MAY	1 ♈	1 ♊ 25 ♋	1 ♈ 21 ♉	1 ♉ 8 ♊	1 ♉ 15 ♊	1 ♓ 6 ♈	1 ♊ 12 ♋	1 ♈ 5 ♉ 29 ♊
JUN	1 ♈ 5 ♉	1 ♋ 19 ♌	1 ♉ 14 ♊	1 ♋ 30 ♌	1 ♊ 8 ♋	1 ♈ 2 ♉ 28 ♊	1 ♋ 8 ♌	1 ♊ 23 ♋
JUL	1 ♉ 8 ♊	1 ♌ 14 ♍	1 ♊ 9 ♋	1 ♊	1 ♋ 2 ♌ 27 ♍	1 ♊ 23 ♋	1 ♌ 9 ♍	1 ♋ 17 ♌
AUG	1 ♊ 5 ♋ 31 ♌	1 ♍ 10 ♎	1 ♋ 3 ♌ 27 ♍	1 ♊ 2 ♋	1 ♍ 21 ♎	1 ♋ 21 ♌	1 ♍	1 ♌ 10 ♍
SEP	1 ♌ 25 ♍	1 ♎ 8 ♏	1 ♍ 20 ♎	1 ♋ 9 ♌	1 ♎ 15 ♏	1 ♌ 11 ♍	1 ♍	1 ♍ 4 ♎ 28 ♏
OCT	1 ♍ 20 ♎	1 ♏ 17 ♐	1 ♎ 14 ♏	1 ♌ 14 ♍	1 ♏ 11 ♐	1 ♍ 5 ♎ 29 ♏	1 ♍	1 ♏ 23 ♐
NOV	1 ♎ 13 ♏	1 ♐ 9 ♏	1 ♏ 7 ♐	1 ♍ 2 ♎ 27 ♏	1 ♐ 7 ♑	1 ♏ 22 ♐	1 ♍ 10 ♎	1 ♐ 16 ♑
DEC	1 ♏ 7 ♐ 31 ♑	1 ♏	1 ♐ 25 ♑	1 ♏ 21 ♐	1 ♑ 7 ♒	1 ♐ 15 ♑	1 ♎ 9 ♏	1 ♑ 11 ♒

♀	1953	1954	1955	1956	1957	1958	1959	1960
JAN	1 ♒ 6 ♓	1 ♑ 23 ♒	1 ♏ 7 ♐	1 ♒ 18 ♐	1 ♒ 13 ♓	1 ♐ 7 ♑	1 ♒	1 ♏ 3 ♐ 28 ♑
FEB	1 ♓ 3 ♈	1 ♒ 16 ♓	1 ♐ 7 ♑	1 ♐ 12 ♑	1 ♓ 6 ♈	1 ♑ 2 ♒	1 ♒	1 ♑ 21 ♒
MAR	1 ♈ 15 ♉	1 ♓ 12 ♈	1 ♑ 5 ♒ 31 ♓	1 ♈ 8 ♉	1 ♒ 2 ♓ 26 ♈	1 ♒	1 ♈ 21 ♉	1 ♒ 16 ♓
APR	1 ♈	1 ♈ 5 ♉ 29 ♊	1 ♓ 25 ♈	1 ♉ 5 ♊	1 ♈ 19 ♉	1 ♒ 7 ♓	1 ♉ 15 ♊	1 ♓ 10 ♈
MAY	1 ♈	1 ♊ 24 ♋	1 ♈ 20 ♉	1 ♊ 9 ♋	1 ♉ 14 ♊	1 ♓ 6 ♈	1 ♊ 11 ♋	1 ♈ 4 ♉ 29 ♊
JUN	1 ♈ 6 ♉	1 ♋ 18 ♌	1 ♉ 14 ♊	1 ♋ 24 ♊	1 ♊ 7 ♋	1 ♈ 2 ♉ 27 ♊	1 ♋ 7 ♌	1 ♊ 22 ♋
JUL	1 ♉ 8 ♊	1 ♌ 14 ♍	1 ♊ 9 ♋	1 ♊	1 ♋ 2 ♌ 27 ♍	1 ♊ 22 ♋	1 ♌ 9 ♍	1 ♋ 16 ♌
AUG	1 ♊ 5 ♋ 31 ♌	1 ♍ 10 ♎	1 ♋ 2 ♌ 26 ♍	1 ♊ 5 ♋	1 ♍ 21 ♎	1 ♋ 16 ♌	1 ♍	1 ♌ 9 ♍
SEP	1 ♌ 25 ♍	1 ♎ 7 ♏	1 ♍ 19 ♎	1 ♋ 9 ♌	1 ♎ 15 ♏	1 ♌ 10 ♍	1 ♍ 21 ♎ 26 ♍	1 ♍ 3 ♎ 28 ♏
OCT	1 ♍ 19 ♎	1 ♏ 24 ♐ 28 ♑	1 ♎ 13 ♏	1 ♌ 7 ♍	1 ♏ 7 ♐	1 ♍ 3 ♎ 28 ♏	1 ♎	1 ♏ 22 ♐
NOV	1 ♎ 12 ♏	1 ♏	1 ♏ 6 ♐	1 ♍ 26 ♎	1 ♏ 6 ♐	1 ♏ 21 ♐	1 ♎ 10 ♏	1 ♐ 16 ♑
DEC	1 ♏ 6 ♐ 30 ♑	1 ♏	1 ♐ 25 ♑	1 ♎ 20 ♏	1 ♐ 7 ♑	1 ♐ 15 ♑	1 ♏ 8 ♐	1 ♑ 11 ♒

♀	1961	1962	1963	1964	1965	1966	1967	1968
JAN	1 ♒ 6 ♓	1 ♑ 22 ♒	1 ♏ 7 ♐	1 ♒ 17 ♓	1 ♐ 13 ♑	1 ♒	1 ♐ 7 ♑ 31 ♒	1 ♏ 2 ♐ 27 ♑
FEB	1 ♓ 3 ♈	1 ♒ 15 ♓	1 ♐ 6 ♑	1 ♓ 11 ♈	1 ♑ 6 ♒	1 ♒ 7 ♓ 26 ♒	1 ♓ 24 ♈	1 ♑ 21 ♒
MAR	1 ♈	1 ♓ 11 ♈	1 ♑ 5 ♒ 31 ♓	1 ♈ 8 ♉	1 ♒ 2 ♓ 26 ♈	1 ♒	1 ♈ 21 ♉	1 ♒ 16 ♓
APR	1 ♈	1 ♈ 4 ♉ 29 ♊	1 ♓ 25 ♈	1 ♉ 5 ♊	1 ♈ 19 ♉	1 ♒ 7 ♓	1 ♉ 15 ♊	1 ♓ 9 ♈
MAY	1 ♈	1 ♊ 24 ♋	1 ♈ 19 ♉	1 ♊ 10 ♋	1 ♉ 13 ♊	1 ♈ 6 ♉	1 ♊ 11 ♋	1 ♈ 4 ♉ 28 ♊
JUN	1 ♈ 6 ♉	1 ♋ 18 ♌	1 ♉ 13 ♊	1 ♉ 18 ♊	1 ♊ 7 ♋	1 ♉ 2 ♊ 27 ♋	1 ♋ 7 ♌	1 ♊ 21 ♋
JUL	1 ♉ 8 ♊	1 ♌ 13 ♍	1 ♊ 8 ♋	1 ♊	1 ♋ 26 ♌	1 ♋ 22 ♌	1 ♌ 9 ♍	1 ♋ 16 ♌
AUG	1 ♊ 4 ♋ 30 ♌	1 ♌ 9 ♍	1 ♋ 26 ♌	1 ♋ 6 ♌	1 ♌ 20 ♍	1 ♋ 16 ♌	1 ♍	1 ♌ 9 ♍
SEP	1 ♌ 24 ♍	1 ♍ 8 ♎	1 ♌ 18 ♍	1 ♋ 9 ♌	1 ♍ 14 ♎	1 ♌ 9 ♍	1 ♍ 10 ♎	1 ♍ 3 ♎ 27 ♏
OCT	1 ♍ 18 ♎	1 ♏	1 ♍ 13 ♎	1 ♌ 6 ♍	1 ♎ 10 ♏	1 ♍ 3 ♎ 27 ♏	1 ♎ 2 ♍	1 ♏ 22 ♐
NOV	1 ♎ 12 ♏	1 ♏	1 ♎ 6 ♏ 30 ♑	1 ♍ 25 ♎	1 ♏ 7 ♐	1 ♏	1 ♎ 10 ♏	1 ♎ 15 ♏
DEC	1 ♏ 6 ♐ 29 ♑	1 ♏	1 ♑ 24 ♒	1 ♎ 20 ♏	1 ♐ 8 ♑	1 ♏ 14 ♐	1 ♏ 8 ♐	1 ♑ 10 ♒

– VENUS TABLES –

♀	1969	1970	1971	1972	1973	1974	1975	1976
JAN	1 ♒ 5 ♓	1 ♑ 22 ♒	1 ♏ 8 ♐	1 ♒ 17 ♓	1 ♐ 12 ♑	1 ♒ 30 ♑	1 ♑ 7 ♒ 31 ♓	1 ♏ 2 ♐ 27 ♑
FEB	1 ♓ 3 ♈	1 ♒ 15 ♓	1 ♐ 6 ♑	1 ♓ 11 ♈	1 ♑ 5 ♒	1 ♑	1 ♓ 24 ♈	1 ♑ 20 ♒
MAR	1 ♈	1 ♓ 11 ♈	1 ♑ 5 ♒ 30 ♓	1 ♈ 8 ♉	1 ♓ 25 ♈	1 ♒	1 ♈ 20 ♉	1 ♒ 15 ♓
APR	1 ♈	1 ♈ 4 ♉ 28 ♊	1 ♓ 24 ♈	1 ♉ 4 ♊	1 ♈ 19 ♉	1 ♒ 7 ♓	1 ♉ 14 ♊	1 ♓ 9 ♈
MAY	1 ♈	1 ♊ 23 ♋	1 ♈ 19 ♉	1 ♊ 11 ♋	1 ♉ 13 ♊	1 ♓ 5 ♈	1 ♊ 10 ♋	1 ♈ 3 ♉ 27 ♊
JUN	1 ♈ 6 ♉	1 ♋ 17 ♌	1 ♉ 13 ♊	1 ♋ 12 ♊	1 ♊ 6 ♋	1 ♉ 26 ♊	1 ♋ 7 ♌	1 ♊ 21 ♋
JUL	1 ♉ 7 ♊	1 ♌ 13 ♍	1 ♊ 7 ♋	1 ♊	1 ♌ 26 ♍	1 ♊ 22 ♋	1 ♌ 10 ♍	1 ♋ 15 ♌
AUG	1 ♊ 4 ♋ 30 ♌	1 ♍ 9 ♎	1 ♌ 25 ♍	1 ♊ 7 ♋	1 ♍ 19 ♎	1 ♋ 15 ♌	1 ♍	1 ♌ 9 ♍
SEP	1 ♌ 24 ♍	1 ♎ 8 ♏	1 ♍ 18 ♎	1 ♋ 8 ♌	1 ♎ 14 ♏	1 ♌ 9 ♍	1 ♌	1 ♍ 2 ♎ 26 ♏
OCT	1 ♍ 18 ♎	1 ♏	1 ♎ 12 ♏	1 ♌ 6 ♍ 31 ♎	1 ♏ 10 ♐	1 ♍ 3 ♎ 27 ♏	1 ♌ 5 ♍	1 ♏ 21 ♐
NOV	1 ♎ 11 ♏	1 ♏	1 ♏ 5 ♐ 30 ♑	1 ♎ 25 ♏	1 ♐ 6 ♑	1 ♏ 20 ♐	1 ♍ 10 ♎	1 ♐ 15 ♑
DEC	1 ♏ 5 ♐ 29 ♑	1 ♏	1 ♑ 24 ♒	1 ♏ 19 ♐	1 ♑ 8 ♒	1 ♐ 14 ♑	1 ♎ 7 ♏	1 ♑ 10 ♒

♀	1977	1978	1979	1980	1981	1982	1983	1984
JAN	1 ♒ 5 ♓	1 ♑ 21 ♒	1 ♏ 8 ♐	1 ♒ 16 ♓	1 ♐ 12 ♑	1 ♒ 24 ♑	1 ♑ 6 ♒ 30 ♓	1 ♏ 2 ♐ 26 ♑
FEB	1 ♓ 3 ♈	1 ♒ 14 ♓	1 ♐ 6 ♑	1 ♓ 10 ♈	1 ♑ 5 ♒ 28 ♓	1 ♑	1 ♓ 23 ♈	1 ♑ 20 ♒
MAR	1 ♈	1 ♓ 10 ♈	1 ♑ 4 ♒ 29 ♓	1 ♈ 7 ♉	1 ♓ 25 ♈	1 ♒	1 ♈ 20 ♉	1 ♒ 15 ♓
APR	1 ♈	1 ♈ 3 ♉ 28 ♊	1 ♓ 23 ♈	1 ♉ 4 ♊	1 ♈ 18 ♉	1 ♒ 7 ♓	1 ♉ 14 ♊	1 ♓ 8 ♈
MAY	1 ♈	1 ♊ 22 ♋	1 ♈ 18 ♉	1 ♊ 13 ♋	1 ♉ 12 ♊	1 ♓ 5 ♈ 31 ♉	1 ♊ 10 ♋	1 ♈ 3 ♉ 27 ♊
JUN	1 ♈ 7 ♉	1 ♋ 17 ♌	1 ♉ 12 ♊	1 ♋ 6 ♊	1 ♊ 6 ♋ 30 ♌	1 ♉ 27 ♊	1 ♋ 7 ♌	1 ♊ 21 ♋
JUL	1 ♉ 7 ♊	1 ♌ 12 ♍	1 ♊ 7 ♋	1 ♊	1 ♌ 25 ♍	1 ♊ 21 ♋	1 ♌ 11 ♍	1 ♋ 15 ♌
AUG	1 ♊ 3 ♋ 29 ♌	1 ♍ 8 ♎	1 ♌ 25 ♍	1 ♊ 7 ♋	1 ♍ 19 ♎	1 ♋ 15 ♌	1 ♍ 28 ♌	1 ♌ 8 ♍
SEP	1 ♌ 23 ♍	1 ♎ 8 ♏	1 ♍ 18 ♎	1 ♋ 8 ♌	1 ♎ 13 ♏	1 ♌ 8 ♍	1 ♌	1 ♍ 2 ♎ 26 ♏
OCT	1 ♍ 17 ♎	1 ♏	1 ♎ 12 ♏	1 ♌ 5 ♍ 31 ♎	1 ♏ 9 ♐	1 ♍ 2 ♎ 26 ♏	1 ♌ 6 ♍	1 ♏ 21 ♐
NOV	1 ♎ 11 ♏	1 ♏	1 ♏ 5 ♐ 29 ♑	1 ♎ 25 ♏	1 ♐ 6 ♑	1 ♏ 19 ♐	1 ♍ 10 ♎	1 ♐ 14 ♑
DEC	1 ♏ 4 ♐ 28 ♑	1 ♏	1 ♑ 23 ♒	1 ♏ 19 ♐	1 ♑ 9 ♒	1 ♐ 12 ♑	1 ♎ 7 ♏	1 ♑ 10 ♒

♀	1985	1986	1987	1988	1989	1990	1991	1992
JAN	1♒ 5♓	1♑ 21♒	1♏ 8♐	1♒ 16♓	1♒ 11♓	1♐ 17♑	1♑ 6♒ 30♓	1♐ 26♑
FEB	1♓ 3♈	1♒ 14♓	1♐ 6♑	1♏ 10♐	1♒ 4♓ 28♈	1♑	1♓ 23♈	1♑ 19♒
MAR	1♈	1♓ 9♈	1♑ 4♒ 29♓	1♈ 7♉	1♓ 24♈	1♑ 4♒	1♈ 19♉	1♒ 14♓
APR	1♈	1♈ 3♉ 27♊	1♓ 23♈	1♉ 17♊	1♈ 17♉	1♒ 7♓	1♉ 13♊	1♓ 17♈
MAY	1♈	1♊ 22♋	1♈ 18♉	1♊ 18♋ 27♊	1♉ 12♊	1♓ 4♈ 31♉	1♉ 9♊	1♈ 2♉ 26♊
JUN	1♈ 7♉	1♋ 16♌	1♉ 12♊	1♉	1♊ 5♋ 30♌	1♉ 25♊	1♋ 7♌	1♊ 20♋
JUL	1♉ 8♊	1♌ 12♍	1♊ 6♋ 31♌	1♊	1♌ 24♍	1♊ 20♋	1♌ 11♍	1♋ 14♌
AUG	1♊ 3♋ 28♌	1♌ 8♍	1♍ 24♎	1♊ 7♋	1♍ 18♎	1♋ 13♌	1♍ 22♎	1♌ 7♍
SEP	1♌ 23♍	1♎ 8♏	1♍ 17♎	1♋ 8♌	1♎ 13♏	1♌ 9♍	1♌	1♎ 25♏
OCT	1♍ 17♎	1♏	1♎ 11♏	1♌ 5♍ 30♎	1♏ 9♐	1♎ 2♏ 26♐	1♍ 7♎	1♏ 20♐
NOV	1♎ 10♏	1♏	1♏ 4♐ 28♑	1♎ 24♏	1♐ 6♑	1♏ 19♐	1♎ 9♏	1♐ 14♑
DEC	1♏ 4♐ 28♑	1♏	1♐ 23♑	1♐ 18♑	1♑ 10♒	1♐ 13♑	1♎ 7♏	1♑ 9♒

♀	1993	1994	1995	1996	1997	1998	1999	2000
JAN	1♒ 4♓	1♑ 20♒	1♏ 8♐	1♒ 15♓	1♐ 10♑	1♑ 10♒	1♑ 5♒ 29♓	1♐ 25♑
FEB	1♓ 3♈	1♒ 13♓	1♐ 5♑	1♓ 9♈	1♑ 4♒ 28♓	1♑	1♓ 22♈	1♑ 19♒
MAR	1♈	1♓ 9♈	1♑ 3♒ 29♓	1♈ 6♉	1♓ 24♈	1♒ 19♓	1♈ 19♉	1♒ 14♓
APR	1♈	1♈ 2♉ 27♊	1♓ 23♈	1♉ 4♊	1♈ 17♉	1♒ 7♓	1♉ 13♊	1♓ 7♈
MAY	1♈	1♊ 21♋	1♈ 17♉	1♊	1♉ 11♊	1♈ 4♉ 30♊	1♊ 9♋	1♈ 2♉ 26♊
JUN	1♈ 7♉	1♋ 15♌	1♉ 15♊	1♊	1♊ 4♋ 29♌	1♊ 25♋	1♋ 6♌	1♊ 19♋
JUL	1♉ 6♊	1♌ 12♍	1♊ 6♋ 30♌	1♊	1♌ 24♍	1♋ 20♌	1♌ 13♍	1♋ 14♌
AUG	1♊ 2♋ 28♌	1♍ 23♎	1♌ 17♍	1♊ 8♋	1♍ 18♎	1♋ 14♌	1♍ 16♎	1♌ 7♍
SEP	1♌ 22♍	1♎ 8♏	1♍ 12♎	1♋ 8♌	1♎ 12♏	1♌ 7♍	1♍	1♎ 25♏
OCT	1♍ 16♎	1♏	1♎ 11♏	1♌ 5♍ 30♎	1♏ 9♐	1♎ 25♏	1♍ 8♎	1♏ 20♐
NOV	1♎ 9♏	1♏	1♏ 4♐ 28♑	1♎ 23♏	1♐ 6♑	1♏ 18♐	1♍ 10♎	1♐ 13♑
DEC	1♏ 3♐ 27♑	1♏	1♑ 22♒	1♏ 17♐	1♐ 12♑	1♐ 12♑	1♎ 6♏	1♑ 9♒

– MARS TABLES –

♂	1921	1922	1923	1924	1925	1926	1927	1928	1929	1930
JAN	1 ♒ 5 ♓	1 ♏	1 ♓ 21 ♈	1 ♏ 19 ♐	1 ♈	1 ♐	1 ♉	1 ♐ 19 ♑	1 ♊	1 ♑
FEB	1 ♓ 13 ♈	1 ♏ 18 ♐	1 ♈	1 ♐	1 ♈ 5 ♉	1 ♐ 9 ♑	1 ♉ 22 ♊	1 ♑ 28 ♒	1 ♊	1 ♑ 6 ♒
MAR	1 ♈ 25 ♉	1 ♐	1 ♈ 4 ♉	1 ♐ 6 ♑	1 ♉ 24 ♊	1 ♑ 23 ♒	1 ♊	1 ♒	1 ♊ 10 ♋	1 ♒ 17 ♓
APR	1 ♉	1 ♐	1 ♉ 16 ♊	1 ♑ 24 ♒	1 ♊	1 ♒	1 ♊ 17 ♋	1 ♒ 7 ♓	1 ♋	1 ♓ 24 ♈
MAY	1 ♉ 6 ♊	1 ♐	1 ♊ 30 ♋	1 ♒	1 ♊ 9 ♋	1 ♒ 3 ♓	1 ♋	1 ♓ 16 ♈	1 ♋ 13 ♌	1 ♈
JUN	1 ♊ 18 ♋	1 ♐	1 ♋	1 ♒ 24 ♓	1 ♋ 26 ♌	1 ♓ 15 ♈	1 ♋ 6 ♌	1 ♈ 26 ♉	1 ♌	1 ♈ 3 ♉
JUL	1 ♋	1 ♐	1 ♋ 16 ♌	1 ♓	1 ♌	1 ♈	1 ♌ 25 ♍	1 ♉	1 ♌ 4 ♍	1 ♉ 14 ♊
AUG	1 ♋ 3 ♌	1 ♐	1 ♌	1 ♓ 24 ♒	1 ♌ 12 ♍	1 ♉	1 ♍	1 ♉ 9 ♊	1 ♍ 21 ♎	1 ♊ 28 ♋
SEP	1 ♌ 19 ♍	1 ♐ 13 ♑	1 ♍	1 ♒	1 ♍ 28 ♎	1 ♉	1 ♍ 10 ♎	1 ♊	1 ♎	1 ♋
OCT	1 ♍	1 ♑ 30 ♒	1 ♍ 18 ♎	1 ♒ 19 ♓	1 ♎	1 ♉	1 ♎ 26 ♏	1 ♊ 3 ♋	1 ♎ 6 ♏	1 ♋ 20 ♌
NOV	1 ♍ 6 ♎	1 ♒	1 ♎	1 ♓	1 ♎ 13 ♏	1 ♉	1 ♏	1 ♋	1 ♏ 18 ♐	1 ♌
DEC	1 ♎ 26 ♏	1 ♒ 11 ♓	1 ♎ 4 ♏	1 ♓ 19 ♈	1 ♏ 28 ♐	1 ♉	1 ♏ 8 ♐	1 ♋ 20 ♊	1 ♐ 29 ♑	1 ♌

♂	1931	1932	1933	1934	1935	1936	1937	1938	1939	1940
JAN	1 ♌	1 ♑ 18 ♒	1 ♍	1 ♒	1 ♎	1 ♒ 14 ♓	1 ♏ 5 ♐	1 ♓ 30 ♈	1 ♏ 29 ♐	1 ♓ 4 ♈
FEB	1 ♌ 16 ♋	1 ♒ 25 ♓	1 ♍	1 ♒ 4 ♓	1 ♎	1 ♓ 22 ♈	1 ♐	1 ♈	1 ♐	1 ♈ 17 ♉
MAR	1 ♋ 30 ♌	1 ♓	1 ♍	1 ♓ 14 ♈	1 ♎	1 ♈	1 ♐ 13 ♏	1 ♈ 12 ♉	1 ♐ 21 ♑	1 ♉
APR	1 ♌	1 ♓ 3 ♈	1 ♍	1 ♈ 22 ♉	1 ♎	1 ♉	1 ♏	1 ♉ 23 ♊	1 ♑	1 ♊
MAY	1 ♌	1 ♈ 12 ♉	1 ♍	1 ♉	1 ♎	1 ♉ 13 ♊	1 ♏ 14 ♐	1 ♊	1 ♑ 25 ♒	1 ♊ 17 ♋
JUN	1 ♌ 10 ♍	1 ♉ 22 ♊	1 ♍	1 ♉ 2 ♊	1 ♎	1 ♊ 25 ♋	1 ♐	1 ♊ 7 ♋	1 ♒	1 ♋
JUL	1 ♍	1 ♊	1 ♍ 6 ♎	1 ♊ 15 ♋	1 ♎ 29 ♏	1 ♋	1 ♐	1 ♋ 22 ♌	1 ♒ 21 ♑	1 ♋ 3 ♌
AUG	1 ♎	1 ♊ 4 ♋	1 ♎ 26 ♏	1 ♋ 30 ♌	1 ♏	1 ♋ 10 ♌	1 ♐ 8 ♑	1 ♌	1 ♑	1 ♌ 19 ♍
SEP	1 ♎ 17 ♏	1 ♋ 20 ♌	1 ♏	1 ♌	1 ♏ 16 ♐	1 ♌ 26 ♍	1 ♑ 30 ♒	1 ♌ 7 ♍	1 ♑ 24 ♒	1 ♍
OCT	1 ♏ 30 ♐	1 ♌	1 ♏ 9 ♐	1 ♌ 18 ♍	1 ♐ 28 ♑	1 ♍	1 ♒	1 ♍ 25 ♎	1 ♒	1 ♍ 5 ♎
NOV	1 ♐	1 ♌ 13 ♍	1 ♐ 19 ♑	1 ♍	1 ♑	1 ♍ 14 ♎	1 ♒	1 ♎	1 ♒ 19 ♓	1 ♎ 20 ♏
DEC	1 ♐ 10 ♑	1 ♍	1 ♑ 28 ♒	1 ♍ 11 ♎	1 ♑ 7 ♒	1 ♎ 7 ♏	1 ♒ 21 ♓	1 ♎ 11 ♏	1 ♓	1 ♏

– MARS TABLES –

♂	1941	1942	1943	1944	1945	1946	1947	1948	1949	1950
JAN	1 ♏ 4 ♐	1 ♈ 11 ♉	1 ♐ 26 ♑	1 ♊	1 ♐ 5 ♑	1 ♋	1 ♑ 25 ♒	1 ♍	1 ♑ 4 ♒	1 ♎
FEB	1 ♐ 17 ♑	1 ♉	1 ♑	1 ♊	1 ♑ 14 ♒	1 ♋	1 ♒	1 ♍ 12 ♌	1 ♒ 11 ♓	1 ♎
MAR	1 ♑	1 ♉ 7 ♊	1 ♑ 8 ♒	1 ♊ 29 ♋	1 ♒ 25 ♓	1 ♋	1 ♒ 4 ♓	1 ♌	1 ♓ 21 ♈	1 ♎ 28 ♍
APR	1 ♑ 2 ♒	1 ♊ 26 ♋	1 ♒ 17 ♓	1 ♋	1 ♓	1 ♋ 22 ♌	1 ♓ 11 ♈	1 ♌	1 ♈ 30 ♉	1 ♍
MAY	1 ♒ 16 ♓	1 ♋	1 ♓ 27 ♈	1 ♋ 22 ♌	1 ♓ 3 ♈	1 ♌	1 ♈ 21 ♉	1 ♌ 18 ♍	1 ♉	1 ♍
JUN	1 ♓	1 ♋ 14 ♌	1 ♈	1 ♌	1 ♈ 11 ♉	1 ♌ 20 ♍	1 ♉	1 ♍	1 ♉ 10 ♊	1 ♍ 11 ♎
JUL	1 ♓ 2 ♈	1 ♌	1 ♈ 7 ♉	1 ♌ 12 ♍	1 ♉ 23 ♊	1 ♍	1 ♊	1 ♍ 17 ♎	1 ♊ 23 ♋	1 ♎
AUG	1 ♈	1 ♍	1 ♉ 23 ♊	1 ♍ 29 ♎	1 ♊	1 ♍ 9 ♎	1 ♊ 13 ♋	1 ♎	1 ♋	1 ♎ 10 ♍
SEP	1 ♈	1 ♍ 17 ♎	1 ♊	1 ♎	1 ♊ 7 ♋	1 ♎ 24 ♏	1 ♋	1 ♎ 3 ♏	1 ♋ 7 ♌	1 ♏ 25 ♐
OCT	1 ♈	1 ♎	1 ♊	1 ♋ 13 ♏	1 ♋	1 ♏	1 ♌	1 ♏ 17 ♐	1 ♌ 27 ♍	1 ♐
NOV	1 ♈	1 ♎ 2 ♏	1 ♊	1 ♏ 25 ♐	1 ♋ 11 ♊	1 ♏ 6 ♐	1 ♌	1 ♐ 26 ♑	1 ♍	1 ♐ 6 ♑
DEC	1 ♈	1 ♏ 15 ♐	1 ♊	1 ♐	1 ♊ 26 ♋	1 ♐ 26 ♑	1 ♍	1 ♑	1 ♍ 26 ♎	1 ♑ 15 ♒

♂	1951	1952	1953	1954	1955	1956	1957	1958	1959	1960
JAN	1 ♒ 22 ♓	1 ♎ 20 ♏	1 ♓	1 ♏	1 ♓ 15 ♈	1 ♏ 14 ♐	1 ♓ 28 ♈	1 ♏	1 ♉	1 ♐ 14 ♑
FEB	1 ♓	1 ♏	1 ♓ 8 ♈	1 ♏ 9 ♐	1 ♈ 26 ♉	1 ♐ 28 ♑	1 ♈	1 ♏ 4 ♐	1 ♉ 10 ♊	1 ♑ 23 ♒
MAR	1 ♓ 2 ♈	1 ♏	1 ♈ 20 ♉	1 ♐	1 ♉	1 ♑	1 ♈ 17 ♉	1 ♐ 17 ♑	1 ♊	1 ♒
APR	1 ♈ 10 ♉	1 ♏	1 ♉	1 ♐ 12 ♑	1 ♉ 10 ♊	1 ♑ 14 ♒	1 ♉ 27 ♊	1 ♑ 27 ♒	1 ♊ 10 ♋	1 ♒ 2 ♓
MAY	1 ♉ 21 ♊	1 ♏	1 ♊	1 ♑	1 ♊ 26 ♋	1 ♒	1 ♊	1 ♒	1 ♋	1 ♓ 11 ♈
JUN	1 ♊	1 ♏	1 ♊ 14 ♋	1 ♑	1 ♋	1 ♒	1 ♊ 21 ♋	1 ♒ 7 ♓	1 ♋ 2 ♌	1 ♈ 20 ♉
JUL	1 ♊ 3 ♋	1 ♏	1 ♋ 29 ♌	1 ♑ 3 ♐	1 ♋ 11 ♌	1 ♒	1 ♋	1 ♓ 21 ♈	1 ♌ 20 ♍	1 ♉
AUG	1 ♋ 18 ♌	1 ♏ 27 ♐	1 ♌	1 ♐ 24 ♑	1 ♌ 27 ♍	1 ♒	1 ♋ 8 ♌	1 ♈	1 ♍	1 ♉ 2 ♊
SEP	1 ♌	1 ♐	1 ♌ 14 ♍	1 ♑	1 ♍	1 ♒	1 ♌ 24 ♍	1 ♈ 21 ♉	1 ♍ 5 ♎	1 ♊ 21 ♋
OCT	1 ♌ 5 ♍	1 ♐ 12 ♑	1 ♍	1 ♑ 21 ♒	1 ♍ 13 ♎	1 ♒	1 ♍	1 ♉	1 ♎ 21 ♏	1 ♋
NOV	1 ♍ 24 ♎	1 ♑ 21 ♒	1 ♍ 20 ♎	1 ♒	1 ♎ 29 ♏	1 ♒	1 ♍ 8 ♎	1 ♉	1 ♏	1 ♋
DEC	1 ♎	1 ♒ 30 ♓	1 ♎ 20 ♏	1 ♒ 4 ♓	1 ♏	1 ♒ 30 ♓	1 ♎ 23 ♏	1 ♉	1 ♏ 3 ♐	1 ♋

♂	1961	1962	1963	1964	1965	1966	1967	1968	1969	1970
JAN	1 ♋	1 ♑	1 ♌	1 ♑, 13 ♒	1 ♍	1 ♒, 30 ♓	1 ♎	1 ♒, 9 ♓	1 ♏	1 ♓, 24 ♈
FEB	1 ♋, 5 ♊, 7 ♋	1 ♑, 2 ♒	1 ♌	1 ♒, 20 ♓	1 ♍	1 ♓	1 ♎, 12 ♏	1 ♓, 17 ♈	1 ♏, 25 ♐	1 ♈
MAR	1 ♋	1 ♒, 12 ♓	1 ♌	1 ♓, 29 ♈	1 ♍	1 ♓, 9 ♈	1 ♏, 31 ♎	1 ♈, 28 ♉	1 ♐	1 ♈, 7 ♉
APR	1 ♋	1 ♓, 19 ♈	1 ♌	1 ♈	1 ♍	1 ♈, 17 ♉	1 ♎	1 ♉	1 ♐	1 ♉, 18 ♊
MAY	1 ♋, 6 ♌	1 ♈, 28 ♉	1 ♌	1 ♈, 7 ♉	1 ♍	1 ♉, 28 ♊	1 ♎	1 ♉, 8 ♊	1 ♐	1 ♊
JUN	1 ♌, 28 ♍	1 ♉	1 ♌, 3 ♍	1 ♉, 17 ♊	1 ♍, 29 ♎	1 ♊	1 ♎	1 ♊, 21 ♋	1 ♐	1 ♊, 2 ♋
JUL	1 ♍	1 ♉, 9 ♊	1 ♍, 27 ♎	1 ♊, 30 ♋	1 ♎	1 ♊, 11 ♋	1 ♎, 19 ♏	1 ♋	1 ♐	1 ♋, 18 ♌
AUG	1 ♍, 17 ♎	1 ♊, 22 ♋	1 ♎	1 ♋	1 ♎, 20 ♏	1 ♋, 25 ♌	1 ♏	1 ♋, 5 ♌	1 ♐	1 ♌
SEP	1 ♎	1 ♋	1 ♎, 12 ♏	1 ♋, 15 ♌	1 ♏	1 ♌	1 ♏, 10 ♐	1 ♌, 21 ♍	1 ♐, 21 ♑	1 ♌, 3 ♍
OCT	1 ♎, 2 ♏	1 ♋, 11 ♌	1 ♏, 25 ♐	1 ♌	1 ♏, 4 ♐	1 ♌, 12 ♍	1 ♐, 23 ♑	1 ♍	1 ♑	1 ♍, 20 ♎
NOV	1 ♏, 13 ♐	1 ♌	1 ♐	1 ♌, 6 ♍	1 ♐, 14 ♑	1 ♍	1 ♑	1 ♍, 9 ♎	1 ♑, 4 ♒	1 ♎
DEC	1 ♐, 24 ♑	1 ♌	1 ♐, 5 ♑	1 ♍	1 ♑, 23 ♒	1 ♍, 4 ♎	1 ♑, 2 ♒	1 ♎, 30 ♏	1 ♒, 15 ♓	1 ♎, 6 ♏

♂	1971	1972	1973	1974	1975	1976	1977	1978	1979	1980
JAN	1 ♏, 23 ♐	1 ♈	1 ♐	1 ♉	1 ♐, 21 ♑	1 ♊	1 ♑	1 ♌, 26 ♋	1 ♑, 21 ♒	1 ♍
FEB	1 ♐	1 ♈, 10 ♉	1 ♐, 12 ♑	1 ♉, 27 ♊	1 ♑	1 ♊	1 ♑, 9 ♒	1 ♋	1 ♒, 28 ♓	1 ♍
MAR	1 ♐, 12 ♑	1 ♉, 27 ♊	1 ♑, 27 ♒	1 ♊	1 ♑, 3 ♒	1 ♊, 18 ♋	1 ♒, 20 ♓	1 ♋	1 ♓	1 ♍, 12 ♌
APR	1 ♑	1 ♊	1 ♒	1 ♊, 20 ♋	1 ♒, 11 ♓	1 ♋	1 ♓, 28 ♈	1 ♋, 11 ♌	1 ♓, 7 ♈	1 ♌
MAY	1 ♑, 3 ♒	1 ♊, 12 ♋	1 ♒, 8 ♓	1 ♋	1 ♓, 21 ♈	1 ♋, 16 ♌	1 ♈	1 ♌	1 ♈, 16 ♉	1 ♌, 4 ♍
JUN	1 ♒	1 ♋, 28 ♌	1 ♓, 21 ♈	1 ♋, 9 ♌	1 ♈	1 ♌	1 ♈, 6 ♉	1 ♌, 14 ♍	1 ♉, 26 ♊	1 ♍
JUL	1 ♒	1 ♌	1 ♈	1 ♌, 27 ♍	1 ♉	1 ♌, 7 ♍	1 ♉, 18 ♊	1 ♍	1 ♊	1 ♍, 11 ♎
AUG	1 ♒	1 ♌, 15 ♍	1 ♈, 12 ♉	1 ♍	1 ♉, 14 ♊	1 ♍, 24 ♎	1 ♊	1 ♍, 4 ♎	1 ♊, 8 ♋	1 ♎, 29 ♏
SEP	1 ♒	1 ♍	1 ♉	1 ♍, 12 ♎	1 ♊	1 ♎	1 ♋	1 ♎, 20 ♏	1 ♋, 25 ♌	1 ♏
OCT	1 ♒	1 ♎	1 ♉, 30 ♈	1 ♎, 28 ♏	1 ♊, 17 ♋	1 ♎, 9 ♏	1 ♋, 27 ♌	1 ♏	1 ♌	1 ♏, 12 ♐
NOV	1 ♒, 6 ♓	1 ♎, 15 ♏	1 ♈	1 ♏	1 ♋, 26 ♊	1 ♏, 20 ♐	1 ♌	1 ♏, 2 ♐	1 ♌, 20 ♍	1 ♐, 22 ♑
DEC	1 ♓, 26 ♈	1 ♏, 30 ♐	1 ♈, 24 ♉	1 ♏, 11 ♐	1 ♊	1 ♐	1 ♌	1 ♐, 13 ♑	1 ♍	1 ♑, 31 ♒

– MARS TABLES –

♂	1981	1982	1983	1984	1985	1986	1987	1988	1989	1990
JAN	1 ♒	1 ♎	1 ♒ 17 ♓	1 ♎ 11 ♏	1 ♓	1 ♏	1 ♓ 8 ♈	1 ♏ 9 ♐	1 ♈ 19 ♉	1 ♐ 30 ♑
FEB	1 ♒ 7 ♓	1 ♎	1 ♓ 25 ♈	1 ♏	1 ♓ 2 ♈	1 ♏ 3 ♐	1 ♈ 20 ♉	1 ♐ 22 ♑	1 ♉	1 ♑
MAR	1 ♓ 17 ♈	1 ♎	1 ♈	1 ♏	1 ♈ 15 ♉	1 ♐ 28 ♑	1 ♉	1 ♑	1 ♉ 11 ♊	1 ♑ 12 ♒
APR	1 ♈ 25 ♉	1 ♎	1 ♈ 5 ♉	1 ♏	1 ♉ 26 ♊	1 ♑	1 ♉ 5 ♊	1 ♑ 6 ♒	1 ♊ 29 ♋	1 ♒ 21 ♓
MAY	1 ♉	1 ♎	1 ♉ 17 ♊	1 ♏	1 ♊	1 ♑	1 ♊ 21 ♋	1 ♒ 22 ♓	1 ♋	1 ♓ 31 ♈
JUN	1 ♉ 5 ♊	1 ♎	1 ♊ 29 ♋	1 ♏	1 ♊ 9 ♋	1 ♑	1 ♋	1 ♓	1 ♋ 16 ♌	1 ♈
JUL	1 ♊ 18 ♋	1 ♎	1 ♋	1 ♏	1 ♋ 25 ♌	1 ♑	1 ♋ 6 ♌	1 ♓ 13 ♈	1 ♌	1 ♈ 13 ♉
AUG	1 ♋	1 ♎ 3 ♏	1 ♋ 14 ♌	1 ♏ 18 ♐	1 ♌	1 ♑	1 ♌ 23 ♍	1 ♈	1 ♌ 3 ♍	1 ♉ 31 ♊
SEP	1 ♋ 2 ♌	1 ♏ 20 ♐	1 ♌ 30 ♍	1 ♐	1 ♌ 10 ♍	1 ♑	1 ♍	1 ♈	1 ♍ 20 ♎	1 ♊
OCT	1 ♌ 21 ♍	1 ♐	1 ♍	1 ♐ 5 ♑	1 ♍ 28 ♎	1 ♑ 9 ♒	1 ♍ 8 ♎	1 ♈ 23 ♓	1 ♎	1 ♊
NOV	1 ♍	1 ♑	1 ♍ 18 ♎	1 ♑ 16 ♒	1 ♎	1 ♒ 26 ♓	1 ♎ 24 ♏	1 ♓ 2 ♈	1 ♎ 4 ♏	1 ♊
DEC	1 ♍ 16 ♎	1 ♑ 10 ♒	1 ♎	1 ♒ 25 ♓	1 ♎ 15 ♏	1 ♓	1 ♏	1 ♈	1 ♏ 18 ♐	1 ♊ 14 ♉

♂	1991	1992	1993	1994	1995	1996	1997	1998	1999	2000
JAN	1 ♉ 21 ♊	1 ♐ 9 ♑	1 ♋	1 ♑ 28 ♒	1 ♍ 23 ♌	1 ♑ 9 ♒	1 ♍ 3 ♎	1 ♒ 25 ♓	1 ♎ 26 ♏	1 ♒ 4 ♓
FEB	1 ♊	1 ♑ 18 ♒	1 ♋	1 ♒	1 ♌	1 ♒ 15 ♓	1 ♎ 6 ♍	1 ♓	1 ♏	1 ♓ 12 ♈
MAR	1 ♊	1 ♒ 28 ♓	1 ♋	1 ♒ 7 ♓	1 ♌	1 ♓ 25 ♈	1 ♍	1 ♓ 5 ♈	1 ♏	1 ♈ 23 ♉
APR	1 ♊ 3 ♋	1 ♓	1 ♋ 28 ♌	1 ♓ 14 ♈	1 ♌	1 ♈	1 ♍	1 ♈ 13 ♉	1 ♏	1 ♉
MAY	1 ♋ 27 ♌	1 ♓ 6 ♈	1 ♌	1 ♈ 24 ♉	1 ♌ 26 ♍	1 ♈ 3 ♉	1 ♍	1 ♉ 24 ♊	1 ♏ 6 ♎	1 ♉ 4 ♊
JUN	1 ♌	1 ♈ 15 ♉	1 ♌ 23 ♍	1 ♉	1 ♍	1 ♉ 12 ♊	1 ♍ 19 ♎	1 ♊	1 ♎	1 ♊ 16 ♋
JUL	1 ♌ 16 ♍	1 ♉ 27 ♊	1 ♍	1 ♉ 3 ♊	1 ♍ 21 ♎	1 ♊ 26 ♋	1 ♎	1 ♊ 6 ♋	1 ♎ 5 ♏	1 ♋
AUG	1 ♍	1 ♊	1 ♍ 12 ♎	1 ♊ 16 ♋	1 ♎	1 ♋	1 ♎ 14 ♏	1 ♋ 21 ♌	1 ♏	1 ♌
SEP	1 ♎	1 ♊ 12 ♋	1 ♎ 27 ♏	1 ♋	1 ♎ 7 ♏	1 ♋ 10 ♌	1 ♏ 29 ♐	1 ♌	1 ♏ 3 ♐	1 ♌ 17 ♍
OCT	1 ♎ 17 ♏	1 ♋	1 ♏	1 ♋ 4 ♌	1 ♏ 21 ♐	1 ♌ 30 ♍	1 ♐	1 ♌ 7 ♍	1 ♐ 17 ♑	1 ♍
NOV	1 ♏ 29 ♐	1 ♋	1 ♏ 9 ♐	1 ♌	1 ♐ 30 ♑	1 ♍	1 ♐ 9 ♑	1 ♍ 27 ♎	1 ♑ 26 ♒	1 ♍ 4 ♎
DEC	1 ♐	1 ♋	1 ♐ 20 ♑	1 ♌ 12 ♍	1 ♑	1 ♍	1 ♑ 18 ♒	1 ♎	1 ♒	1 ♎ 23 ♏